# CONTENTS

# INTRODUCTION

Caves are fascinating places that invite all sorts of questions. Where does the dark passage lead? How deep is that hole and can we reach the bottom? Where does the water go?

Caving allows you to explore gigantic **chambers** with impressive waterfalls and amazing mineral **formations**, and there is always the chance that you might discover somewhere no one has been before. Caving combines skills such as climbing, swimming and map reading, but you don't have to be super-fit to take part, because there are different grades of caves – some are difficult to descend and some are easy.

This well-equipped caver is placing his feet carefully as he follows the water in a **streamway**.

# DIFFERENT NAMES

- **Caver**  someone who explores caves for sport.

- **Potholer**  a caver who explores potholes (caves with a vertical entrance).

- **Speleologist**  someone who explores and studies caves for science.

- **Spelunker**  an untrained and poorly equipped person who has entered a cave.

# Radical Sports

# CAVING

Chris Howes ···········

www.heinemann/library.co.uk
Visit our website to find out more information about Heinemann Library books.

To order:
☎ Phone 44 (0) 1865 888066
🖹 Send a fax to 44 (0) 1865 314091
🖥 Visit the Heinemann Library Bookshop at www.heinemann/library.co.uk to browse our catalogue and order online.

First published in Great Britain by Heinemann Library,
Halley Court, Jordan Hill, Oxford OX2 8EJ,
a division of Reed Educational and Professional Publishing Ltd.
Heinemann is a registered trademark of Reed Educational & Professional Publishing Limited.

OXFORD  MELBOURNE  AUCKLAND
JOHANNESBURG  BLANTYRE  GABORONE
IBADAN  PORTSMOUTH NH (USA)  CHICAGO

Designed by Celia Floyd
Illustrations by Jeff Edwards (p18) and Rhian Hicks (p23)
Originated by Universal
Printed in Hong Kong by Wing King Tong

ISBN 0 431 03690 X
06 05 04 03 02
10 9 8 7 6 5 4 3 2 1

**British Library Cataloguing in Publication Data**

Howes, Chris, 1951–
 Caving. – (Radical sports)
 1. Caving  Juvenile literature
 I. Title
 796.5'25

**Acknowledgements**

The Publishers would like to thank the following for permission to reproduce photographs: All photographs Chris Howes/Wild Places Photography, except Stockfile, p12a.

Cover photograph reproduced with permission of Chris Howes/Wild Places Photography.

Our thanks to Caving Supplies of Buxton, UK, for loan of equipment, and to Jane Bingham for her help in the preparation of this book.

Every effort has been made to contact copyright holders of any material reproduced in this book. Any omissions will be rectified in subsequent printings if notice is given to the Publisher.

This book aims to cover all the essential techniques of this radical sport but it is important when learning a new sport to get expert tuition and to follow any manufacturers' instructions. Never enter a cave on your own or without having gained suitable experience.

## A short history

For centuries, caves have attracted visits by people wanting to satisfy their curiosity. **Archaeologists** have uncovered animal bones and the remains of prehistoric people in caves. Tourists have marvelled at the wonders that lie beneath the earth.

No one person can be said to have 'invented' caving but, in 1888, the Frenchman Édouard Martel began exploring caves for sport as well as study. He visited England in 1895 and, using a rope ladder, descended the vast 110m deep shaft of Gaping Gill in Yorkshire, succeeding where others had failed. This exciting feat triggered a new interest in exploring caves for their own sake, and caving as a sport grew and spread around the world.

This drawing is of Édouard Martel using a rope ladder to descend the vast entrance shaft of Gaping Gill in 1895.

## Caving today

Caves are found in virtually every country of the world. Many are easy to find near roads or even in towns, but some lie high on mountains or deep in jungles. Others are hidden so well that no one has found them yet. Thousands of people take part in the sport, simply because exploring caves is exciting and fun!

# Getting Started

Caving is a very safe sport when approached with care. Modern cavers use specialist clothing and equipment to make exploring caves safer, but there are also rules that must be followed. One of the most basic rules is that you must never enter a cave on your own – if you have even a minor accident, such as a twisted ankle, you will need help.

Everyone can go caving – it is a sport for all ages and all sizes. You don't have to be small and thin to be a caver. However, you will need training before you can go caving. You will learn some things underground, but a lot of training will take place on the surface.

## Where can I train?

Most young people start caving with their school. They may go on a course run at an outdoor pursuits centre that offers a range of sports. Scouts and similar groups also run courses. Some newcomers to the sport are first taken underground by a parent or friend who already goes caving – it is worth asking if your family knows anyone suitable.

You will need training before you descend a cave on a rope.

# Top Tip

- Caving is not a competition where you have to be the fastest person and beat your friends to the finish line. Move at your own pace while underground. You are there to discover a new world, not to race to the other end of the cave.

An indoor climbing wall with a caving instructor is an excellent choice for learning ropework skills. Artificial training caves have been built in some regions and these give a good idea of what the real thing will be like. They include **squeezes**, climbs and even water and **formations**.

Some caving clubs offer surface training, although there may be a minimum age so younger members will usually need to be accompanied by an adult. The national caving organization in your country (see page 31) can put you in contact with your nearest caving instructor or club.

## Teamwork

Teamwork is very important in caving so groups of between four and six cavers usually work together. This means that there are enough people to help others through difficult sections of the cave and to carry equipment which will be used by everyone.

Caves are formed by water, so experienced cavers expect to find streams and waterfalls.

# YOUR PERSONAL KIT

Your choice of clothing will depend on the type of cave you are exploring. Some caves are draughty and wet with water flowing through them, while others can be dry and dusty. Although caves stay much the same temperature all year round, this can be cold or warm depending on where you are in the world. Take the advice of your instructor when you prepare for your caving expedition.

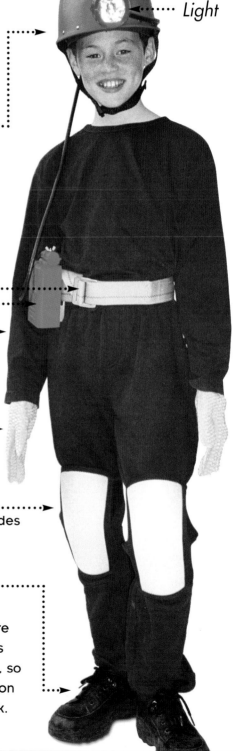

*Light*

### Helmet
Your helmet will protect you if you fall or hit your head on a passage roof. It also protects your head from falling stones.

*Belt*

### Battery for light

### Old clothes
Old clothes are suitable for easy, dry caves.

### Gloves
Gloves can help to protect your hands from abrasion, though many cavers do not wear gloves at all.

### Kneepads
Good kneepads are essential to protect you when you crawl over rocks. Make sure you have the right size: too tight prevents easy movement and too loose slides down your leg. Sometimes cavers also wear elbow pads.

### Boots
The best boots for caving are made from man-made material and have eyelets for laces. Quick-lace hooks are dangerous as they can catch on wire ladders. Your boots should have good ankle support and soles that grip well, so training shoes are unsuitable. Many cavers wear wellington boots, but check that these have a good grip on wet rock.

The best choice of clothes for easy, **dry caves** is usually something old that you don't mind getting muddy, wet or torn. Outer clothing should be loose fitting to allow freedom of movement – a one-piece overall is a good choice. Do not wear denim jeans as these can be tight, cold and clammy when wet.

## Helmet

A good-quality caving helmet is vital. Ensure that the helmet is comfortable and does not fall over your eyes when you move – the cradle inside is adjustable. Only use a helmet designed specifically for caving; never use an industrial 'hard hat', as it will not fully protect you in a fall.

## Safety Standard mark

Caving helmets and other specialist equipment will carry a UIAA or CE sticker or badge showing that it is made to an international standard.

## Lights

There are several types of caving light, all of which clip onto the helmet so that you can keep both hands free. Rechargeable batteries are carried on the back of the helmet or on a belt, and can power the latest **LED lights** for many hours. Some lights produce a beam while others, like LED lights, give a very even light. Try caving with different types before you decide which to buy.

# EXTRA EQUIPMENT

Cavers wear special clothing in caves that are cold or wet. Protective oversuits and undersuits help to keep cavers warm, even if they have been in water. However, if you have to be in wet conditions for a long time, a wetsuit is the best choice of clothing.

## Undersuit

This well-equipped caver is wearing a one-piece undersuit manufactured from stretchy man-made fleece material. Water drains quickly and the fleece remains warm even when wet.

## Oversuit

Oversuits are hard wearing and waterproof and have a built-in hood which folds away when not in use. Most heat is lost through the head so, in cold caves, wear the hood underneath your helmet. Oversuits are made in one piece to keep water out and avoid catching on rocks.

## Harness

A caving harness is used to attach a **lifeline** when making climbs, and is used for **SRT**.

## Cave pack

A cave pack or tackle sack is used to carry gear such as ladders, ropes, climbing equipment and a first aid kit that will be used by the team.

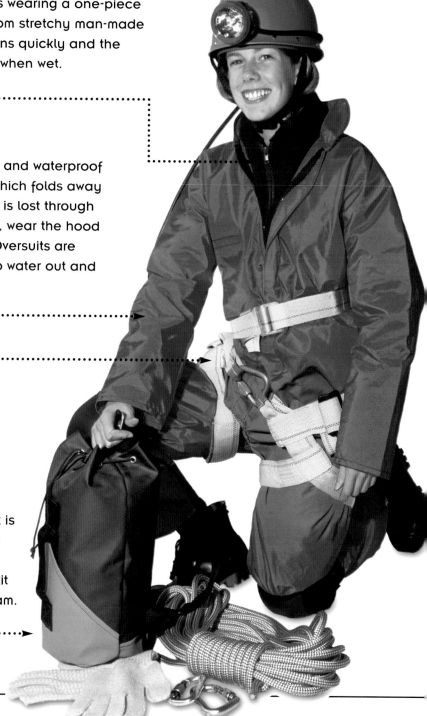

This caver is in very wet conditions and is wearing a wetsuit.

## Wetsuit

Wetsuits are made of a rubber called **neoprene**, which helps you to float as well as keeping you warm. A wetsuit should fit snugly; water will still creep in, but it soon warms up next to your skin.

## Carrying your kit

As well as ropes and other team equipment, cavers carry water, food, a spare light (or two!), plus extra batteries and bulbs. To avoid having many separate packs to carry, these might be added to the team's tackle sack or a smaller, personal pack. Tackle sacks and packs used in caving are smooth and do not have many straps so there are fewer parts to catch on rocks. Because you are part of a team, you may end up carrying your friends' kit and they will help with yours – everyone takes a turn.

Wearing the correct gear – an undersuit and waterproof oversuit – will help when tackling demanding situations.

# CHECKS AND PREPARATIONS

## Keeping fit

You are not in a race while you are underground so there is nothing to stop you having a rest if you need it. However, you will need stamina – the ability to keep going for a long time, perhaps for many hours. You will also need to be supple in order to fit through narrow **squeezes**.

## The right food

You should eat a healthy diet to stay fit – how much energy you have depends on the types of food you eat. When you are exercising, eat energy-rich meals that are high in **carbohydrates** such as cereals or porridge, pasta, rice or potatoes.

Take plenty of exercise between caving trips – jogging, cycling and swimming are all sports that help build suppleness and stamina.

### Taking food underground

Some trips underground will last for several hours, so you will need to take food and drink with you. Avoid carrying heavy, bulky food, as you may have to travel through very narrow passages. Do not be tempted to take only chocolate and sugary foods – although these provide a quick burst of energy, their effects soon wear off. Good choices are dried fruit, such as apricots, or energy bars.

Take plenty of liquid to drink – it is important not to become **dehydrated**. Carry drinks in a plastic bottle (never glass, it might break in a squeeze), or buy small drink cartons with a straw attached. These can be squashed flat afterwards so they are smaller to carry out.

A sheet of polythene or cooking foil is useful – spread it out while you are eating to catch crumbs. You should never leave any trace of where you have been, as even small particles of food can upset the delicate balance of life found in caves.

## Checking the weather
Some caves are unsafe to visit during unsettled weather. Rain that has fallen a week before can sometimes unexpectedly cause a cave to flood. If it has been raining, or if rain is forecast, you should put off your trip until another day or explore a drier cave.

## Staying in touch
Always tell somebody where you have gone and how long you will be, and remember to telephone when you are out of the cave so that everyone knows that the team is safe. Don't forget to take money for the phone.

## SAFETY FIRST

When you prepare for your trip, ensure your kit is in good condition – you will rely on it while underground. Take care of your equipment – repair any tears in clothing, recharge your batteries and check that your light works properly. Make sure spares, such as batteries and bulbs, are also in good condition.

Cave entrances can be horizontal or vertical (vertical entrances are sometimes called **potholes**). Never approach a vertical entrance without being tied to a rope, as it may be unfenced with a sloping or slippery edge.

## The underground experience

Cave passages twist, turn and change shape from small and narrow to tall and wide – so you need different techniques to travel through them. Most people think of caves as always being tight and nasty, but this is far from true as they may contain huge **chambers** or caverns.

These two cave entrances are very different. A caver is forced to squeeze into the entrance above, but the one below is easily large enough to walk into.

# SAFETY UNDERGROUND

- Never attempt anything that you are not happy with. You might be nervous the first time you try to pass a squeeze – don't be afraid to ask for help.

- Keep thinking – don't just follow the person in front.

## Crawling and squeezing

However large the passage is, sooner or later you will find a place where it narrows or boulders block the way. You will have to **crawl** or **squeeze** through a small space to where the passage becomes larger again.

Before you enter a small hole in a cave, look to see whether it twists and heads upwards or downwards. If the hole goes downwards it is easier and safer to enter it feet first.

## A good choke

If there are many fallen rocks in a heap that fills the passage this may be part of a **boulder choke**. You might think that boulders can fall anywhere at any time in a cave, but this is unlikely – caves have been there for millions of years and are very stable. However, always take care in a boulder choke in case any rocks are loose – they might not fall on you, but they can still wobble and roll.

When a passage is particularly low you have to lie down and wriggle – cavers call this a flat-out crawl.

## TOP TIP

- Passage floors are rarely flat. Sometimes passages are clean-washed by water, but others may be covered in sand, mud or boulders. You must watch where you place every footstep to avoid slipping on mud or tripping over a loose rock. Even a minor fall underground can be serious.

## Traversing

Sometimes cavers want to avoid travelling along the floor of a passage, perhaps because it is full of water or covered in boulders. If the passage is the right shape and size cavers can use a technique called traversing.

## Coping with water

Sooner or later you will get very wet, perhaps when following the route the water takes as it flows down a passage. Sometimes cavers have to cross deep pools so if you cannot swim, tell your instructor.

When a passage roof lowers until it almost meets a water surface, this forms a duck – a place where there is hardly any air space and you have to duck through to the other side. Even if you are wearing a wetsuit, do not underestimate how cold the water can be. Cavers often lie on their back to go through a duck, so that they can keep their noses in the air.

To **traverse** in a passage with good footholds, place one foot and one hand on either wall and 'walk' along the passage, legs astride. In narrower passages use your back on one wall and both feet on the other.

# SAFETY FIRST

- Only enter the water when and where your instructor tells you it is safe.

- Never enter a **duck** without supervision.

- Leave **sumps** to the cave diver!

This caver is in a duck. Because he planned ahead, he knew he would need to wear a wetsuit.

A sump forms where the passage is totally filled with water. This is the domain of the cave diver, a very specialised type of caver. Even tackling a duck requires great care and only the most experienced cavers take up cave diving.

# GRADING CAVES

- Although there is always the chance to discover a totally new part of a cave, most passages have already been explored. The best route to take and what equipment is needed will be detailed in a cavers' guidebook, so that cavers can plan their trip.

- Caves are graded according to difficulty. There is no international scale of grades but, in general, a low number indicates an easy cave and a high number shows a hard one. Grades can only be a rough guide to difficulty. What a tall person finds easy a short one will not, and vice versa.

| Grade 1 | Easy cave | No **pitches** (vertical drops) or difficulties |
| Grade 2 | Moderate | May include small climbs or pitches |
| Grade 3 | Difficult | Some sections require stamina, but there are no particular hazards |
| Grade 4 | Severe | Hazardous sections present, such as large pitches or long **crawls** |
| Grade 5 | Very severe | Very strenuous with mixed hazards such as wet pitches; rescue may be difficult or impossible |

# USING A LIFELINE

A rope is used for protection when on a climb, so that if you fall you are supported and cannot hit the ground. The rope used in climbing will stretch a little if this happens, which means that it absorbs the force of the fall without hurting the caver. Because it protects your life, this rope is called a **lifeline**.

## Tying the knot

Before cavers can use a lifeline, they must attach it to themselves. To do this a figure-of-eight knot is tied in the end of the lifeline.

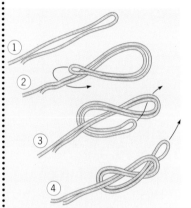

1
2
3
4

Practise tying a figure-of-eight knot until you can do so perfectly, even in total darkness. Add an overhand knot to ensure it cannot come undone.

figure-of-eight knot

overhand knot

screwgate karabiner

snapgate karabiner

## Clipping in

The lifeline is attached to the caver's harness, which may be carried in the **tackle sack** until it is needed. The harness is worn around the waist and legs and the figure-of-eight knot is attached to the front of the harness using a **karabiner** – this is called clipping in. There are different types of karabiners: always use a screwgate karabiner and close it securely so that it cannot open by mistake.

## Belaying

The other end of the rope is held by another caver who is called the **belayer**. The rest of the team takes it in turn to make the climb, while the belayer holds the lifeline. The belayer is protected from falling by using a rope that attaches to an **anchor** point on the cave wall, perhaps a handy rock or a hole that the rope can be threaded through. For safety, two or three anchors are used together in case one gives way. The belayer feeds the rope in or out as required by the climbing caver, so that there is no slack in the rope and the caver cannot fall more than a few centimetres.

This caver is using a rope to descend a **pitch**.

## Caring for your rope

Lives depend on the quality of the lifeline. Never stand on a rope, as you may force grit and mud into it, which causes damage and weakens the lifeline. Clean ropes thoroughly after use and hang them up to dry.

## SAFETY FIRST

🦇 Have your harness and knots checked by someone experienced until you are sure you have everything correct. With practice, it will become second nature to prepare and clip onto the rope.

# GOING VERTICAL

A cave passage can suddenly turn into a vertical drop or **pitch**, which you have to find a way down. Of course, coming in the other direction, you have to climb up in order to move onwards. The techniques involved are called descending and ascending.

## Ladder and line

For short pitches, cavers sometimes use a flexible ladder made from wire cables and metal rungs. Wire ladders are normally about 7m long but they can be linked together for longer drops. Practise climbing up and down a ladder before you go underground. Support your weight on your legs, not your arms, and climb using both hands and one foot behind the ladder, hooking in with your heel – this helps to keep you upright. To prevent you from falling while you use a ladder, a **lifeline** is attached to your harness.

## Single Rope Technique

On long pitches cavers use the Single Rope Technique (**SRT**). The technique uses a single rope, which cavers climb up using **ascenders** or slide down using a **descender**.

An SRT rope is very different from a lifeline. During SRT, the caver travels along the rope, so it has to withstand a lot of rubbing.

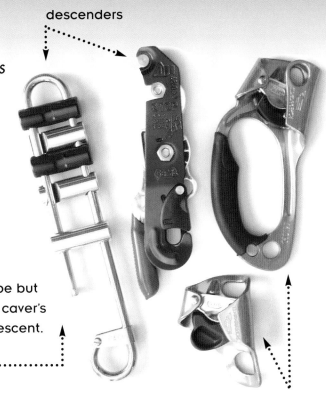

descenders

ascenders

## Ascenders and descenders

To climb up a rope, cavers use two ascenders. These slide upwards along the rope but then grip it so they cannot slide back down. By alternately putting weight on one ascender while the other is moved up, a caver can climb in safety.

To descend – or **abseil** – cavers are attached to the rope using a single descender. This grips the rope but allows it to slide through under the caver's control, so that you make a slow descent.

For safety reasons, a lifeline needs to stretch a little when a caver falls while attached to it, but if an SRT rope stretched the caver would bounce up and down while ascending it. To avoid bouncing, SRT ropes are very tough and hardly stretch at all.

Practise SRT on the surface before trying it underground. SRT is extremely safe and great fun when the technique is carried out correctly, but you should only ever try it with an instructor.

## SRT SAFETY

🦇 Use a screwgate **karabiner** and ensure it is locked.

🦇 Use the right type of rope – never use a lifeline for **SRT** or an SRT rope as a lifeline.

🦇 Experienced cavers have died by being careless. Don't be one of them – check all your equipment before you start.

🦇 Train, train some more – then enjoy yourself!

# FINDING YOUR WAY

## Reading the cave

You should always know where you are in a cave. Sometimes a passage looks the same in both directions – especially after you have taken a rest and forgotten which way you came in. Some areas of a cave may be like a maze, so how do you know which is the way out? Cavers do not leave trails of paper or unravel balls of string to follow; they take note of their surroundings and know where they are at all times. Everyone has to know the way out in case someone else on the team, including the instructor, has an accident.

Use natural features to help, such as whether you are travelling down-slope or up-slope. Are you moving with or against the flow of water? As you pass a junction, turn and look back: this is what you will see when you return, so remember what it looks like.

Cave **formations** such as **stalactites** or **stalagmites** form landmarks that will help you to remember the way.

## Mapping the cave

Cavers make maps (also called surveys) of caves to help with planning the trip. Maps indicate hazards and are useful for route finding. A good map will give clues that cavers use to help them find new passages.

There are many types of cave map ranging from a very basic one sketched from memory, which you could do yourself after your first trip, to a very accurately drawn map produced after the cave is measured using a compass and measuring tape.

# A cave map

Maps have symbols to show some of the obstacles. Cavers use the information to plan a route and work out what equipment they might need.

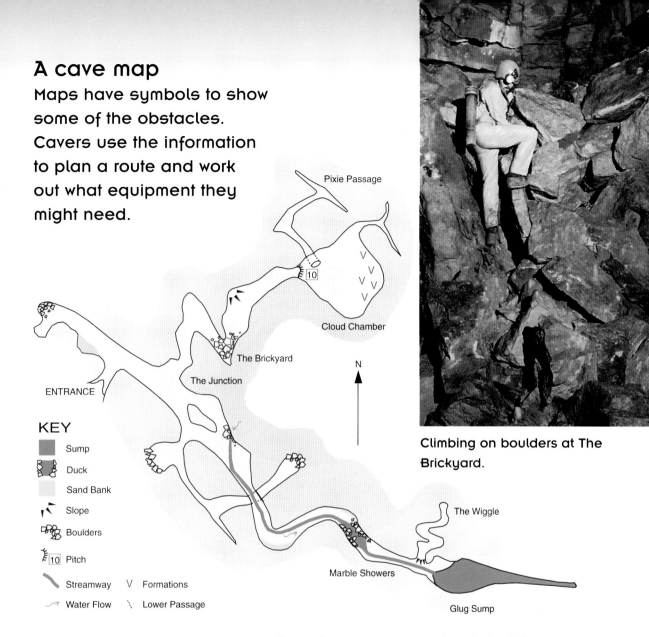

Climbing on boulders at The Brickyard.

Pixie Passage

Cloud Chamber

The Brickyard

The Junction

ENTRANCE

N

## KEY

| | |
|---|---|
| ▨ | Sump |
| ▨ | Duck |
| ▨ | Sand Bank |
| ⌒ | Slope |
| ⬡ | Boulders |
| 10 | Pitch |
| ⟋ | Streamway |
| V | Formations |
| ⟋ | Water Flow |
| ⋱ | Lower Passage |

The Wiggle

Marble Showers

Glug Sump

Imagine you are going into this cave. From The Junction you have two choices – follow the water or go through a **boulder choke** at The Brickyard. Following the water means you would need a wetsuit to pass through the **duck** and your trip ends at a **sump**. You need **SRT** kit to pass the **pitch** on the other route, but you can reach Cloud Chamber filled with **formations**.

The duck at Marble Showers.

# SAFETY UNDERGROUND

## Working together

Caving is a team sport – you help others and they help you. The team should move at the speed of its slowest member, which might be a different person in different types of passage, so always make sure that the caver behind you is not falling behind. Do not force anyone to move faster than they are comfortable with and slow down if you feel you are moving too fast for safety. Make sure you never separate from the group and always follow the instructor's advice.

A tired caver is more likely to have an accident, so take even more care near the end of a trip. If you are tired, then tell the instructor – eating energy food or taking a break might be the answer. Watch for anyone else who appears tired and always be prepared to turn back before you have reached where you intended to go – it might be a long way back to the surface.

These cavers are working together by using a dinghy to safely cross deep water in a French cave.

# If things go wrong

Every sport has things that go wrong, but in caving even a minor problem can quickly become a major one. Teams should carry a basic first-aid kit and everyone must know how to use it. Attending a first-aid course is a good idea.

Other emergencies can arise. After heavy rain or when snow is melting, some caves can completely fill with water, though it is more likely that only a short section of passage will fill up. This can temporarily trap an unwary party beyond a **sump**. If you have planned your trip properly this will not happen to you, but if it does you will have to wait until the passage drains once more. If you are trapped in a cave do everything you can to help yourself, for example by staying warm and dry.

Take extra care in fast-flowing water.

If a member of your team is severely injured, no less than two cavers should go to the surface to raise the alarm. If a team is lost or delayed, the alarm will be raised when you do not return on time.

## SAFETY FIRST

- Take breaks when you need them.
- Eat properly – take suitable food.
- If you are cold or tired, tell your **leader**.

# YOU AND THE CAVE

So you've been caving and you want to progress. You will improve your skills simply by going caving and by taking courses – especially for techniques such as **SRT**. There is probably a caving club nearby, where cavers can advise on the latest gear and where to find the best caves.

All caving trips have a purpose. Often this is to learn more about the cave, such as how it formed. There are always questions to be answered, such as where the water flows to after it has disappeared into a **sump** or finding the best place to look for new passages.

Cavers develop specialities within the sport and study some aspect of caving that fascinates them. Any interest you have can be applied to caving, from biology to photography. Learning more about the underground world is an important and fascinating part of caving.

Formations are delicate: look but never touch!

## Conserving the cave

Caves are not sporting playgrounds; they are formed by nature and are 'non-renewable' – that is, we cannot make more caves if we damage the ones we have. Do your part to keep the cave as it is now: never drop litter and watch where you place every footstep. Some areas with **formations** or untouched mud floors may be protected by **conservation tape**, which serves as a warning not to get too close. Touching formations such as **stalactites** and **stalagmites** can damage them, because oil from your skin stops the formation from growing.

Footpaths may be lined with conservation tape – do not cross one for any reason.

Never leave any sign that you have been in the cave – it should remain the same for the next team to discover and explore.

## Bats

Some types of bats live in caves. These wonderful animals will not harm you, but they may die if they are disturbed, so never approach or handle a bat. To ensure that bats are given a safe place to live, some caves have a gate across the entrance to keep people out but allow bats to fly through.

# YOUR RESPONSIBILITY

- Take nothing but pictures; do not even leave footprints.
- Respect the cave and the animals that live in it.
- Carry out everything you brought in.

Caves are found in nearly every country of the world – wherever there is **limestone**, there are caves. Because one of the driving forces of caving is exploration, expeditions regularly set out to discover new caves in uncharted regions. This makes caving a truly international sport with literally hundreds of thousands of caves to visit.

Wonderful formations decorate this chamber in Carlsbad Caverns.

## North America

Cavers in the USA have a multitude of caves to seek out. The area bounded by Tennessee, Alabama and Georgia is known as TAG Country (after the initials of the states) and offers lots of scope for **SRT**. Some national parks are based on caves, for example Mammoth Cave in Kentucky and New Mexico's Carlsbad Caverns.

A caver (circled) shows the huge size of this entrance at Jenolan.

## Australasia

One of the most important caving regions in Australia is Tasmania, which is famous for its deep systems. The mountains near Sydney hold classic areas such as Jenolan and Bungonia. The flat plains of the Nullarbor contain long, shallow, flooded caves that are explored by divers. Over 7000 caves have so far been discovered in Australia. New Zealand has two major caving regions – Waitomo on North Island and Nelson on South Island.

## Asian attractions

In Sarawak, on the island of Borneo, Gunung Mulu National Park is famous for Sarawak Chamber. Discovered in 1981 by British cavers, it is the world's largest known **chamber** at 600m long and 415m wide – that's big enough to contain twenty football pitches.

## European depths

Europe has a wide range of caves, including most of the world's deepest caves, as well as caves high on mountains that contain permanent ice **formations**. In France, caving is considered a major sport. The Gouffre Berger in France is a deep cave that is visited each year by international expeditions.

The major cave regions of the British Isles lie in the Yorkshire Dales, the Peak District, South Wales, the Mendip hills, and in Ireland in Co. Fermanagh and Co. Clare, but there are also many smaller areas.

## Into the record book

The longest known cave in the world is Mammoth Cave in the USA, which is 530km long. In January 2001, Krubera cave in the Caucasus mountains of Georgia in central Asia became the deepest known cave when its explorers descended to an amazing 1710m below the surface.

These formations are in a cave in South Wales which was discovered in 1994. Over 64km of passage have already been explored.

# GLOSSARY

**abseil**   technique used to slide safely down a rope using friction to slow the descent

**anchor**   attachment point for a rope, often a bolt or suitably shaped rock (also known as a belay point)

**archaeologist**   person who studies prehistoric remains, which are often found in caves

**ascender**   device attached to an SRT rope that slides upwards and grips the rope

**belaying**   technique of holding a rope to protect a climber from falling

**boulder choke**   section of cave filled (choked) with fallen boulders

**carbohydrates**   foods that the body uses for energy

**chamber**   part of a cave that is larger than the passages leading to and from it

**choke**   section of cave filled with fallen boulders

**conservation tape**   plastic tape used to mark areas that cavers should not enter

**crawl**   low section of cave that forces you to use your hands and knees

**dehydrated**   a condition when you have less water in your body than you should

**descender**   device attached to a rope that allows a caver to slide downwards under control

**dry cave**   cave without flowing water in a stream or river, though it may still be wet and muddy with occasional pools

**duck**   passage where water nearly touches the roof, only leaving a small air space

**formation**   general term for stalactites, stalagmites and similar deposits that grow in caves

**handline**   rope that can be pulled on to help cross or climb a difficult section of cave

**karabiner**   strong metal clip used to attach a rope to an anchor or harness

**leader**   experienced person in each caving team who best knows the cave

**LED light**   light made with light-emitting diodes, which lasts for many hours from one set of batteries

**lifeline**   safety rope to prevent a climber falling

**limestone**   rock in which most caves are formed

**neoprene**   rubber material used to make wetsuits, gloves and socks

**pitch**   vertical drop requiring equipment to climb up or down it

**pothole**   cave with a vertical entrance

**showcave**   a cave visited by tourists, usually with concrete floors and electric lights

**squeeze**   small or tight section of cave

**SRT**   Single Rope Technique, used for ascending or descending a vertical drop

**stalactite**   cave formation growing downwards from the ceiling

**stalagmite**   cave formation growing upwards from the floor

**streamway**   cave passage with a flowing stream or river

**sump**   flooded section of a cave with no air space

**tackle sack**   bag used to carry kit such as ropes and SRT equipment

**traverse**   horizontal move across a vertical drop, perhaps along a ledge

**wet cave**   cave that contains flowing water, such as a stream or river

# USEFUL ADDRESSES

*Suppliers of equipment, books and videos, and professional cave leaders/trainers, can be contacted via advertisements in magazines or links from websites.*

British Cave Research Association
The Old Methodist Chapel
Great Huxlow, Buxton
Derbyshire, SK17 8RG

National Caving Association
Monomark House
27 Old Gloucester Street
London, WC1N 3XX

Speleological Union of Ireland
c/o AFAS, House of Sport
Longmile Rd, Walkinstown
Dublin, Republic of Ireland

## Australasia

Australian Speleological Federation
PO Box 388, Broadway
NSW 2007, Australia

New Zealand Speleological Society
PO Box 18
Waitomo Caves, North Island
New Zealand

# FURTHER READING

## Books

*Guidebooks listing known caves in many regions of the world are available through equipment outlets.*

*Adventure of Caving,* David McClurg
(D & J Press)

*Caving Practice & Equipment,* David Judson
(ed) (BCRA)

*The Complete Caving Manual,* Andy Sparrow
(Crowood Press)

*Radical Sports: Rock climbing,* Neil Champion
(Heinemann Library)

## Magazines

*Caves and Caving,* quarterly (BCRA, UK)

*Descent,* bimonthly (Wild Places Publishing, UK)

## Videos

*Cave Safe,* a series of three videos on caving skills (Third Eye Films)

## Websites

www.caves.org.au
Australian Speleological Federation

www.caving.uk.com
*Descent* magazine, equipment suppliers, club contacts and general information

www.nca.org.uk
National Caving Association (UK)

www.cavingireland.org
Speleological Union of Ireland

rubens.its.unimelb.edu.au/~pgm/uis
Union Internationale de Spéléologie: the international speleology site

www.cavepage.magna.com.au/cave/cave.html
International links

All the Internet addresses (URLs) given in this book were valid at the time of going to press. However, due to the dynamic nature of the Internet, some addresses may have changed, or sites may have ceased to exist since publication. While the author and publishers regret any inconvenience this may cause readers, no responsibility for any such changes can be accepted by either the author or the publishers.

# INDEX

# Titles in the *Radical Sports* series include:

Hardback       0 431 03695 0

Hardback       0 431 03690 X

Hardback       0 431 03692 6

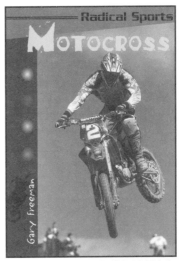

Hardback       0 431 03691 8

Hardback       0 431 03694 2

Hardback       0 431 03693 4

Find out about the other titles in this series on our website www.heinemann.co.uk/library